ZING HUMAN BODY

DIGESTIVE SYSTEM

GRETCHEN HOFFMANN

 Marshall Cavendish
Benchmark

Marshall Cavendish Benchmark
99 White Plains Road
Tarrytown, New York 10591
www.marshallcavendish.us

Text copyright © 2009 by Marshall Cavendish Corporation

All Web sites were available and accurate when this book was sent to press.

Editor: Karen Ang
Publisher: Michelle Bisson
Art Director: Anahid Hamparian
Series Designer: Kay Petronio

Library of Congress Cataloging-in-Publication Data
Hoffmann, Gretchen.

Digestive system / by Gretchen Hoffmann.
p. cm. — (The amazing human body)
Includes bibliographical references and index.
Summary: "Discusses the parts that make up the human digestive system, what can go wrong, how to treat those illnesses and diseases, and how to stay healthy"—Provided by publisher.
ISBN 978-0-7614-3058-2
1. Digestive organs—Juvenile literature. I. Title. II. Series.
QP145.H56 2009
612.3—dc22
2008017573

 = cells from the pyloric region of the stomach

Front cover: The human digestive system

Title page: Diverticulosis, a condition in which pouches form in the walls of parts of the large intestine

Back cover: Sections of the mucous membrane that line the stomach

Photo research by Tracey Engel

Front cover: Purestock / SuperStock
The photographs in this book are used by permission and through the courtesy of: Photo Reseachers, Inc.: David Gifford, 4; Anatomical Travelogue, 7; Biophoto Associates, 17; SPL, 28; Dr. Tim Evans, 33; Profs. P. M. Motta, T. Fujita, & M. Muto, 36; VEM, 40; Scimat, 43; Du Cane Medical Imaging Ltd., 44; AJPhoto, 45; Brian Evans, 52. Alamy: Nucleus Medical Art, Inc., 6, 18, 22, 25, 27, 46, 51; MedicalRF.com, 13, 39, 54; PHOTOTAKE Inc., 14, 16, 20; Krzysztof Szpil , 37; Steven May, 57; Medical-on-Line, 58, 62; D. Hurst, 60; Bubbles Photolibrary, 61; David Young-Wolff, 64; Blend Images, 65. Shutterstock: Sebastian Kaulitzki, 8; Pichugin Dmitry, 65; George Bailey, 67; Kiselev Andrey Valerevich, 68; RCPPHOTO, 69; Jump Photography, 70. Custom Medical Stock Photo: SPL, 10, back cover; M. English, MD, 1, 49. Getty Images: 3D4Medical.com, 12; Nucleus Medical Art, Inc., 24, 56; Dr. Richard Kessel, 31. Superstock: Image Source, 15

Printed in China
123456

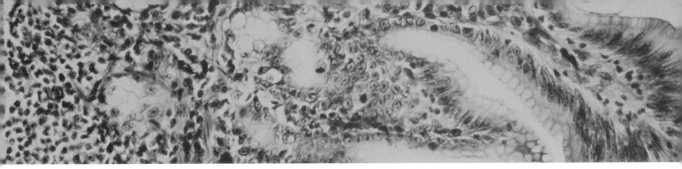

CONTENTS

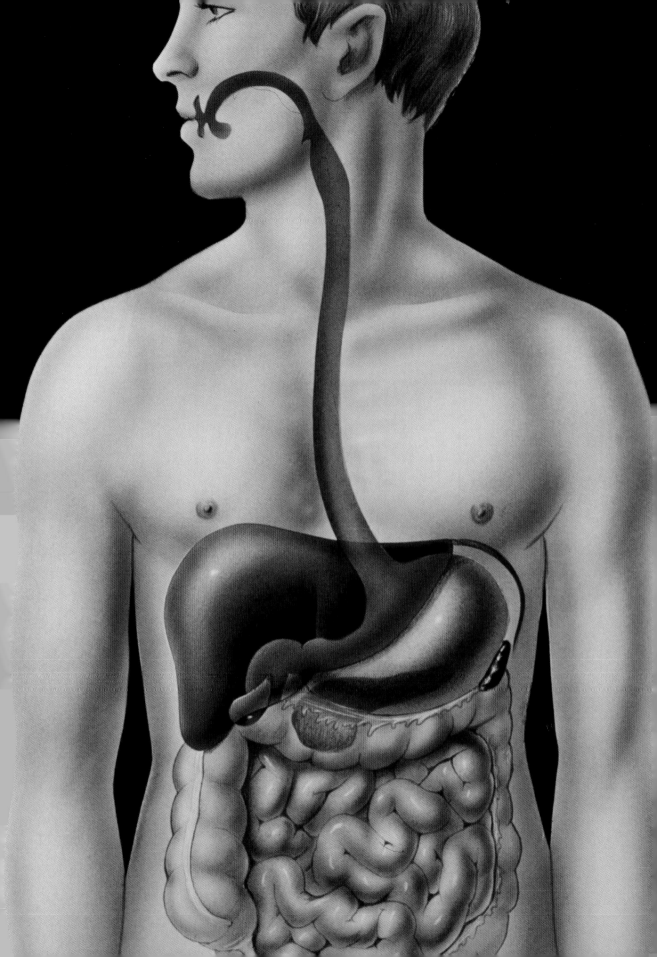

What Is the Digestive System?

The nutrients in food—such as carbohydrates, vitamins, proteins, fats, and minerals—provide the body's cells with the energy and materials it needs for work, growth, and repair. The problem is that most of these nutrients cannot be used by the body for energy in the form in which they are eaten. They are locked inside the food and must be broken out and changed into smaller, usable pieces before they can be absorbed and carried to cells throughout the body.

This is the job of the digestive system—to break down, or digest, the food we eat into their smallest parts. These parts will then be used as energy for existing cells and to build new cells. There are four basic

The digestive system is made up of a collection of organs and other internal body parts.

stages of the digestive process, and the entire cycle usually takes one to two days to complete.

The first step is ingestion, when food and drink is taken into the body through the mouth. The next step is digestion, which involves the physical mixing and grinding of food, the chemical breakdown of the large molecules of food into smaller molecules, and the movement of the meal through the digestive tract. Absorption is the next step, when nutrient molecules taken up by the digestive tract are passed into the bloodstream so that they can be carried throughout the body. The final step is egestion, when the undigested food and waste is removed from the body in the form of feces.

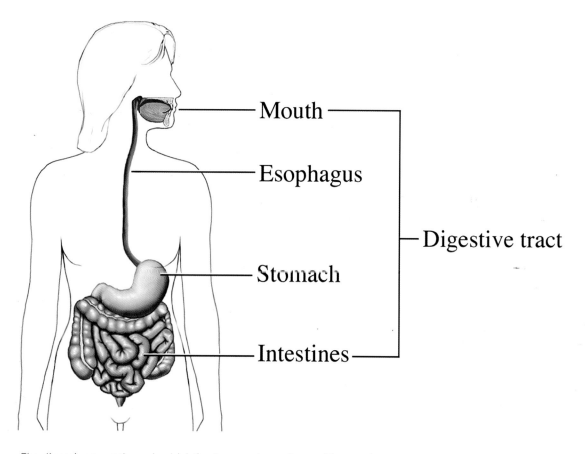

Mouth

Esophagus

Digestive tract

Stomach

Intestines

The digestive tract through which food moves is made up of four main parts.

MANY ORGANS WORKING TOGETHER

The digestive process is a complicated task carried out by many organs working together in the digestive system. The main organs that make up the digestive system form a tube that connects the place that food comes in (the mouth) with the exit point for digested food leaving the body (the anus). This network, known as the gastrointestinal tract or the alimentary canal, is made up of the mouth, throat, esophagus, stomach, small intestine, and large intestine.

Digestion begins in the mouth, where food is chewed and swallowed. Salivary glands in the mouth produce saliva to lubricate the food and to start the chemical breakdown of food. From the mouth, food travels

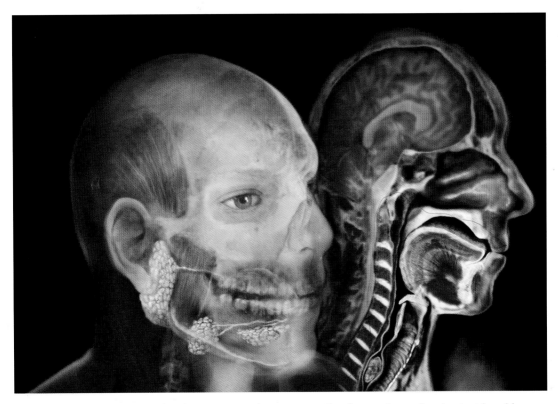

Digestion begins in the mouth, where your teeth, tongue, and saliva work together to start breaking down the food.

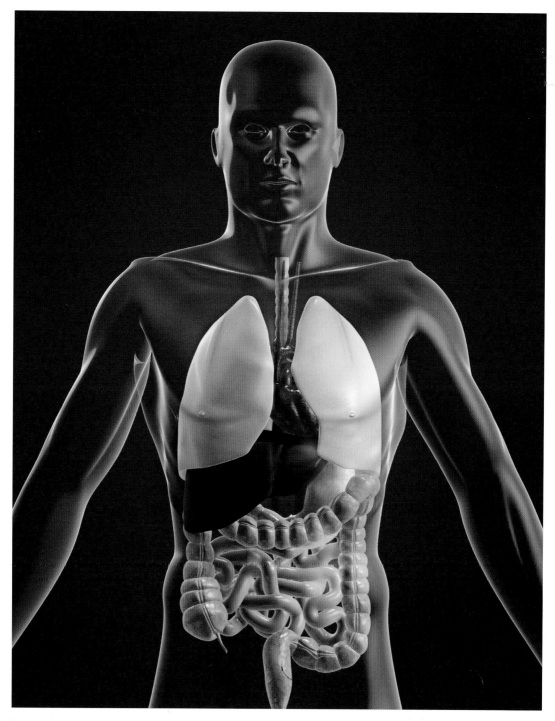

In order to break down food, the digestive system also relies on organs, fluids, and tissues from other body systems.

through the esophagus to the stomach. The stomach temporarily stores the food eaten at each meal. In the stomach, food is further broken down by powerful muscle contractions and by acidic juices. The food is now in a mushy liquid form, and it travels to the small intestine. Even though the food has already been partially processed by the mouth and stomach, the small intestine does the most work of any digestive organ. This is where the food is broken down by physical grinding and also by special proteins called enzymes that work on food at the molecular level. The small intestine is also where almost all of the useful nutrients are absorbed into the body. By the time what is left of the meal reaches the large intestine, almost all of the nutritionally useful products have been removed. All that is left of the undigested food is waste. The main job of the large intestine is to absorb water back into the body and to store the waste until it is excreted from the body. Together, the small and large intestine are often called the bowels.

There are also other organs that are not part of the twisted tube through which food travels that play important roles in the digestive system. The liver, pancreas, and gallbladder assist in digestion by providing digestive juices and enzymes that pour into the small intestine through connective tubes. In addition, the liver processes and stores nutrients once they have been absorbed. Parts of other organ systems, such as nerves and blood, also play a major role in the digestive process.

How the Digestive System Works

The digestive system pulls out all the useful materials from the food we eat as it pushes the food along through the twists and turns of the alimentary canal. Each organ in the digestive system has a special and important role to play in the digestive process.

THE MOUTH

The mouth is the entrance of the digestive system where food is ingested and digestion begins. The mouth is made up of several parts, including the top and bottom jaw bones, the roof (called the palate), the tongue, and the teeth.

This magnified image—which has been colored—shows the mucous membranes that line the insides of the stomach.

As you chew your food, the teeth cut each bite into smaller and smaller pieces. Humans have thirty-two teeth—sixteen on the upper jaw and sixteen on the lower jaw. When you smile in a mirror, you can see that your teeth are various shapes and sizes throughout your mouth. You may also notice that they are arranged in matching pairs, starting in the front and working their way toward the back. The teeth toward the back of the mouth are bigger and wider than the smaller, thinner ones toward the front. That is because different types of teeth have different roles. The four teeth that are front and center on each jaw are the incisors, meant for slicing and cutting through the food. On either side of the incisors are the canine teeth. The four canines are helpful to stab through food to help grip and tear off pieces. Next are the premolars and molars— five on the left and right side of both jaws making a total of twenty. These teeth are

Your jaws and teeth work together with the salivary glands (shown in yellow and red) to start the digestive process.

designed to crush, grind, and mash the food before it is swallowed.

Teeth are not the only way food is prepared for digestion in the mouth. The teeth get help from the tongue and the watery, slimy liquid called saliva. Saliva is produced by the salivary glands. There are six major salivary glands—three on both sides of the mouth and throat. These salivary glands make saliva and release it into the mouth through many small tubes called salivary ducts. The salivary ducts empty into the mouth near the upper teeth and under the tongue on the floor of the mouth. In addition to the three pairs of large salivary glands, there are tiny salivary glands lin-

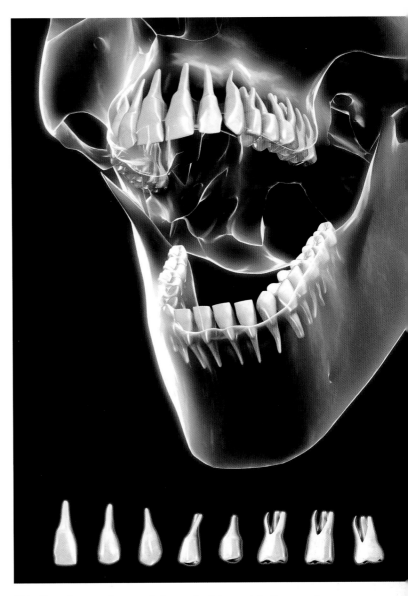

This X-ray image shows a full set of adult teeth in the mouth (top) and the different shapes that teeth can have (bottom).

ing the inside of the lips, cheeks, mouth, and throat. Saliva helps protect your teeth from decay and makes the mouth moist. It also helps begin digestion in the mouth because saliva contains an enzyme that starts to break down starch, which is a major part of many foods such as vegetables, rice, wheat, corn, and potatoes.

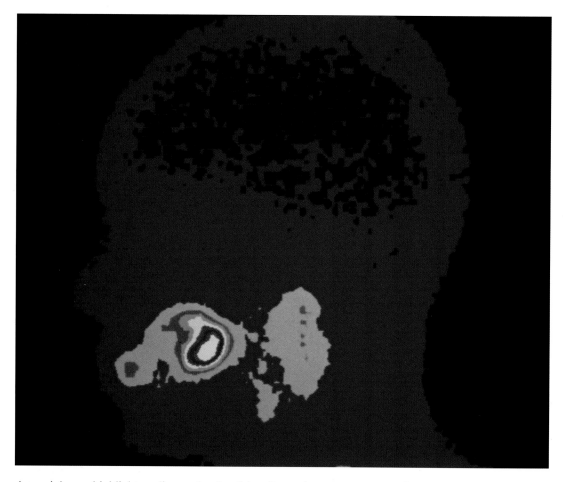

A special scan highlights salivary gland activity. Even when you are not eating, you produce saliva. It helps coat and protect your mouth and teeth.

The muscular tongue helps move food around the mouth while chewing and mixes the food with saliva. After the teeth and saliva have turned the bite of food into a soft mash, the tongue pushes the chewed food against the back of the mouth where it touches the sides and back of the throat. This triggers the swallowing reflex. The throat does not really have a specialized role in digestion. The lining of the throat does produce a little bit of saliva, but its main job is to connect the mouth with the esophagus.

THE ESOPHAGUS

Once food has been chewed and mixed with saliva in the mouth, it is swallowed and passes down the esophagus. The esophagus is the tube that connects the mouth with the stomach. In an adult, the esophagus is approximately 10 inches (25.4 centimeters) long and is made up of layers of muscle. The inside of the esophagus is lined by the mucosal layer to help the food slide along. It takes approximately four to eight seconds for most types of food to travel from the throat through the esophagus to the stomach. For very soft foods or liquids, the journey takes less than a second.

WHAT IS A MUCOSAL LAYER?

The organs of the gastrointestinal tract are lined inside with a protective layer called the mucosal layer or mucosa. In the mouth, esophagus, stomach, and small intestine, the mucosa contains glands that produce juices to help digest food. The mucosal layer protects that walls of the organ from damage. In the small intestine it also helps in the absorption of nutrients. Without the mucosa, the digestive juices would start to digest the organs themselves and the food would not slide through the digestive tract easily.

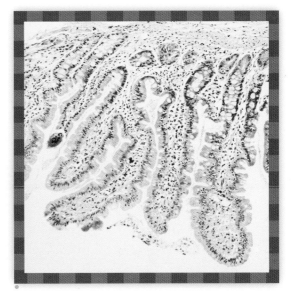

Samples of the mucosa found in the jejunum, a part of the small intestine.

THE STOMACH

The stomach is an expandable pouch shaped like the letter "J." It is located on the left side of the abdominal cavity. When it is empty, the stomach is quite small and has the capacity to hold only about 1/4 cup (.06 liters) of liquid. But after a meal, the stomach stretches and the volume can increase to 1 gallon (3.8 l). This amazing ability to expand comes from the folds in the stomach wall. When empty, the walls of the stomach are folded and compact, but after a meal, the stomach walls stretch out using all of that extra tissue that was folded up. It is almost like the way an accordion is pushed together and folded up, but can be stretched out.

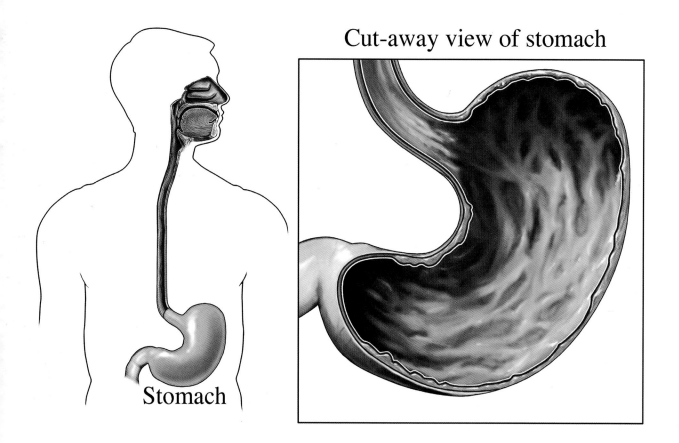

Cut-away view of stomach

Stomach

The stomach has several important jobs. It produces juices that digest food and also kill any potentially harmful bacteria in the food. Gastric juice contains hydrochloric acid that activates certain digestive enzymes and also kills bacteria. The lining of the stomach is filled with millions of glands that produce this acidic gastric juice. These glands produce acid when food arrives in the stomach. But the glands also release the acid when you simply see, smell, or think about food. The mucosal layer lining the stomach protects it from being digested by its own acidic juices.

Additionally, the stomach has three layers of muscle in its walls. These muscles work to crush and squeeze the food into a paste. By grinding food into smaller particles and mixing it with digestive juices, the food can be absorbed when it reaches the small intestine.

The stomach also controls the rate at which food leaves and enters the small intestine. The stomach temporarily stores food for a few hours while the digestive process takes place. Without this pause in the process, the body would not be able to digest and absorb food fast enough to keep up with ingestion. Normally, it takes

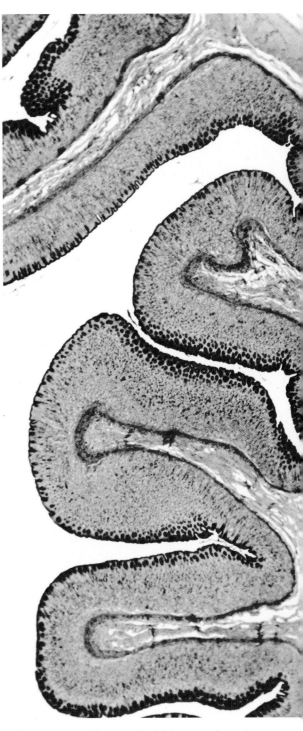

A tissue sample displays the folded muscle and gastric glands that line the stomach.

about two hours for most of an average-sized meal to leave the stomach. The time it takes depends on what was eaten, because different types of food empty from the stomach at different rates. Foods containing a lot of fat, such as fried foods, take longer to leave the stomach than low-fat foods, such as fruits and vegetables.

SMALL INTESTINE

Several hours after eating a meal, the food has traveled through the grinding gate of the mouth, down the tube of the esophagus, and through the squeezing stomach. It has been turned into an unrecognizable, almost

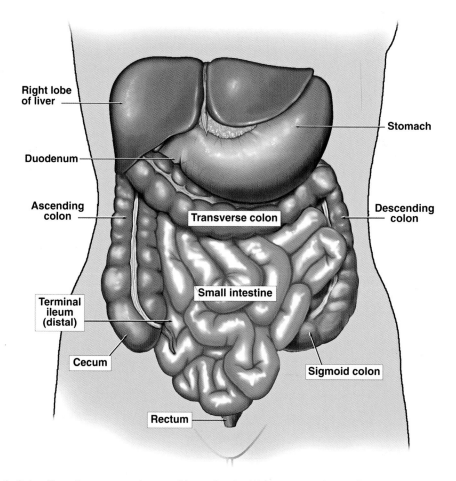

Out of all the digestive organs, the small intestine is the longest and most important part.

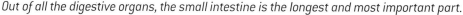

liquid paste called chyme. But it has yet to reach the most important part of the digestive tract—the small intestine. The small intestine is the longest and most important section of the alimentary canal because most of the chemical and mechanical digestion is done there. It is also where almost all of the useful nutrients in the food are absorbed.

The small intestine is called "small" because it is narrower than the final portion of the intestines, the large intestine. The small intestine is approximately 1 inch (2.5 cm) in diameter, compared with the average 3-inch (7.6 cm) diameter of the large intestine. There is nothing small, however, about the length of the small intestine. Inside the body, it is coiled and folded to fit inside the abdomen (the space between the chest and the hips), but the small intestine would be approximately 20 feet (6.1 meters) long if it was stretched out to its full length.

There are three main sections to the small intestine. The duodenum is the first and shortest of the three sections. It receives food from the stomach and its main job is to neutralize the stomach acid so that the food paste can be further digested. The middle section is called the jejunum. The final section is the ileum, which is the longest section. The jejunum and ileum twist and turn their way through the lower part of the abdomen.

Like the esophagus and stomach, the small intestine is lined with a mucosal layer. The mucosa of the small intestine has several special features that help maximize digestion and absorption. First, the mucosal layer of the small intestine has many ridges and folds. These folds are called plicae. These folds have tiny fingerlike branches that stick out to grab even more food particles. These little projections are called villi. The villi themselves are covered in a forest of even smaller hairs called microvilli. There are more than 200 million microvilli per square millimeter of the lining of the small intestine. This network of folds and projections increases the amount of surface that the food can touch inside the small intestine. Providing more opportunities for food to make contact with the walls of the small intestine helps the organ digest food and absorb all the nutrients possible.

The small intestine produces its own intestinal fluid, and it also receives digestive juices produced by the pancreas and liver. These juices break down the complex food molecules into smaller, simple parts that can be absorbed and used by the body. Nutrients are absorbed through the cells of the villi and are passed into the bloodstream.

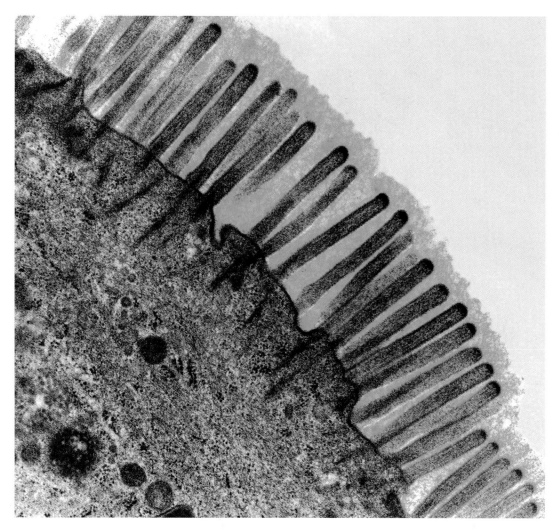

This colored micrograph shows the tiny microvilli found in the small intestine.

The small and large intestines are coiled and packed inside the abdominal cavity. While the digestive action is happening on the inside of the intestinal tube, the outside of the intestines rub against other organs, muscles, and the folded parts of the intestines themselves. To prevent the intestines from sticking together inside the abdomen, the outside layer called serosa is very smooth—unlike the ridges of the inner mucus layer.

LARGE INTESTINE

By the time digestive products reach the large intestine, almost all of the nutritionally useful products have been removed. The primary role of the large intestine is to absorb water and prepare the waste to be expelled from the body. Approximately 3 to 5 gallons (11 to 19 l) of fluid flow into the large intestine every day. This fluid is a combination of the liquids that we drink and the digestive juices that are secreted to help with food absorption. Most of this fluid is reabsorbed in the large intestine to prevent dehydration (excessive water loss in the body).

There are four sections of large intestine—the cecum, the colon, the rectum, and the anal canal. The first section is the cecum, which is the short section that connects to the end of the small intestine. The next and longest section is the colon. The colon loops around the inside of the abdomen and has several subsections. The ascending colon travels up

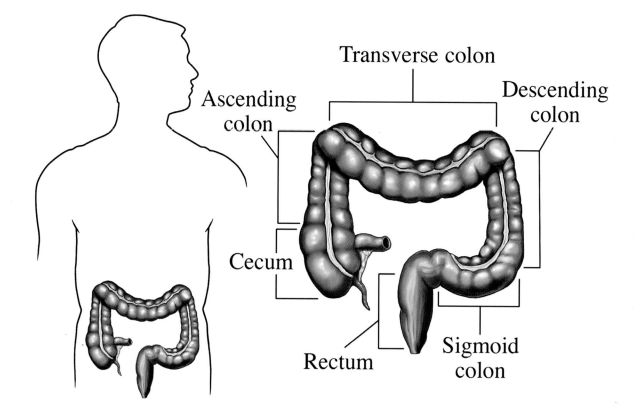

Transverse colon

Descending colon

Ascending colon

Cecum

Rectum

Sigmoid colon

Each part of the large intestine plays an important role in digesting food and excreting waste.

from the point where it is connected to the cecum. Next, the transverse colon leads from the right side of the body to the left. The next subsection of the colon, the descending colon, travels down the left side of the body toward the last section. The colon's last section is the S-shaped sigmoid colon. Solid waste, also called feces or stool, is stored in the sigmoid colon. The waste passes to the next section of the large intestine, which is called the rectum. The feces are then pushed into the final section called the anal canal before reaching the anus. This is the opening through which solid waste exits, where it is pushed out of the body. This final process of expelling waste is egestion, also called defecation or, more commonly, pooping. It is also called a bowel movement. Defecation is considered normal if feces hold together, contain no blood, and pass easily without pain or cramping.

Feces are made up of mostly fiber and undigested food. But they also contain intestinal cells that have died and been rubbed off the intestinal wall and bacteria. Billions of bacteria live in the large intestine. Inside the body, many types of bacteria are helpful and do not cause illness. Outside the body, however, they can be harmful. Washing your hands after going to the bathroom is important because it helps prevent spreading these bacteria to food and to other people, which can cause illness.

There are several organs that are part of the digestive system but are not part of the tube-like pathway that food follows through the body.

PANCREAS

The pancreas is a large gland located behind the stomach. The pancreas produces digestive juices and enzymes that are released into the small intestine. Pancreatic juices balance the acid from the stomach and make the contents of the small intestine less acidic. A variety of pancreatic enzymes are responsible for breaking down starch, proteins, and fats.

Another job of the pancreas is to regulate the levels of sugar in the blood by producing insulin. Insulin is a hormone that controls the level of sugar in the body. It travels through the body in the blood. The body needs to keep a strict level of sugar in the blood for energy. Very high or very low levels of blood sugar can be very dangerous.

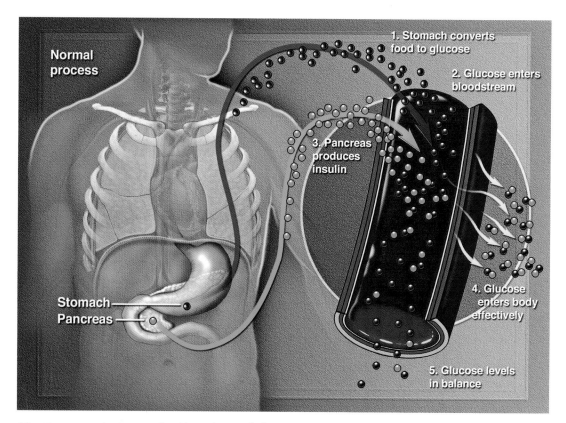

Normal process

1. Stomach converts food to glucose

2. Glucose enters bloodstream

3. Pancreas produces insulin

4. Glucose enters body effectively

5. Glucose levels in balance

Stomach

Pancreas

After the stomach changes food into glucose (1), the glucose enters the bloodstream (2). Working together with the brain and other organs, the pancreas produces insulin (3) that helps to keep glucose levels in check (4 and 5). Abnormal glucose levels can cause problems or illnesses like diabetes.

LIVER

The liver is the largest internal organ. It can weigh more than 3 pounds in an adult. It is located on the right side of the body under the ribs. The liver plays several important roles in the digestive system. The liver processes nutrients once they have been absorbed. Nutrients taken out of food are transported through the bloodstream to the liver where they can be stored, distributed to cells around the body, or broken down into even smaller parts. The liver stores many vitamins and minerals needed for processes throughout the body. It also filters toxins, poisons, and drugs from the blood. The liver also produces bile, a greenish liquid that turns fats into

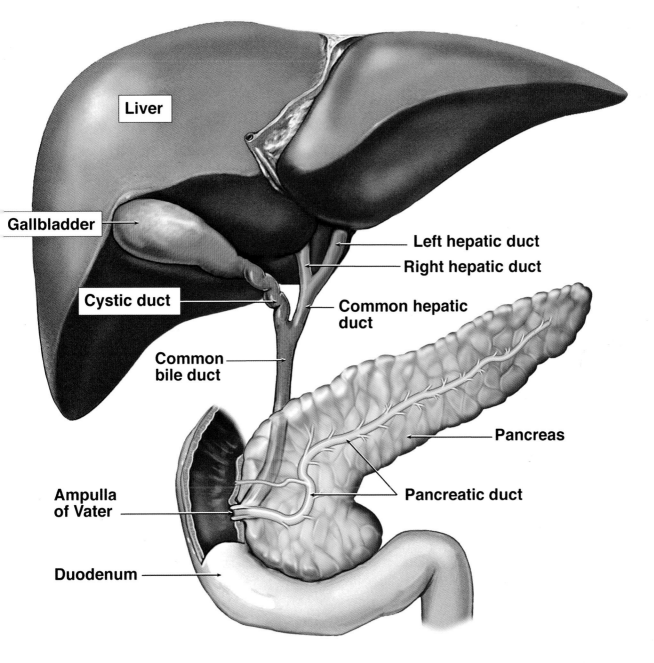

Liver

Gallbladder

Left hepatic duct

Right hepatic duct

Cystic duct

Common hepatic duct

Common bile duct

Pancreas

Pancreatic duct

Ampulla of Vater

Duodenum

Some digestive fluids from the liver, pancreas, and gallbladder travel through ducts—or vessels—to the duodenum, the first part of the small intestine.

small droplets and makes the job of fat-digesting enzymes easier. While bile is produced by the liver, it is actually stored in the gallbladder.

GALLBLADDER

The gallbladder is a storage pouch for bile produced by the liver. It is tucked into a small indentation on the lower end of the liver and is connected to the liver and to the small intestine by small tubes called ducts. Bile is squeezed into the small intestine by the gallbladder through the bile duct. This tube connects with another duct from the pancreas called the pancreatic duct. Bile mixes with pancreatic juices and enzymes before emptying into the first part of the small intestine, the duodenum.

HOW FOOD MOVES THROUGH THE DIGESTIVE SYSTEM

The large, hollow organs of the digestive system have very strong, muscular walls that can squeeze together, expand, or pulse to mix, grind, or push food along. Swallowing is the first important movement that involves the muscles of the tongue, throat, and esophagus. This process of swallowing food starts by choosing to swallow. But once swallowing starts it cannot be stopped because it is a reflex and nerves automatically take control. The muscular walls of the throat squeeze together, or contract, and push the food down into the esophagus. To keep food from entering the trachea (also called the windpipe, the tube that brings air to the lungs), a special barrier called the epiglottis closes off the opening of the trachea during the swallowing reflex.

Next, the food moves down the esophagus, driven by muscle contractions and helped by gravity. In the esophagus, the inner layer of muscle squeezes like a fist and forces the food down into the next section

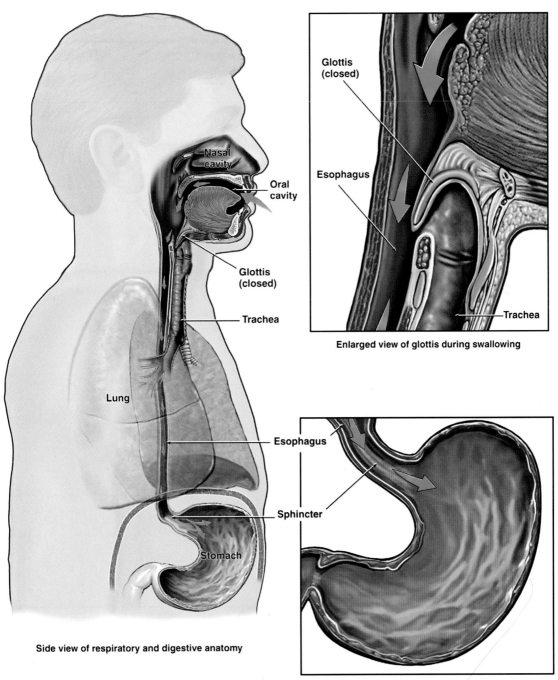

Glottis
(closed)

Esophagus

Trachea

Enlarged view of glottis during swallowing

Nasal
cavity

Oral
cavity

Glottis
(closed)

Trachea

Lung

Esophagus

Sphincter

Stomach

Side view of respiratory and digestive anatomy

Enlarged view of full stomach

When you swallow (upper right), the epiglottis closes off the glottis—the opening of your trachea, or windpipe. This prevents food from traveling down your trachea and into your lungs. Specialized muscles, called sphincters, help move food down through the digestive canal (bottom right).

of the tube toward the stomach. When one section of the esophagus squeezes tight, the next section relaxes and expands to allow the food to move along. This series of contracting and expanding to move the food is known as peristalsis. This is how food moves through the esophagus, stomach, and intestines.

When food empties into the stomach from the esophagus, the walls of the stomach contract and release to mix the food with the digestive juices and also to physically grind the food into smaller pieces. It also controls the release of food and liquid into the small intestine. The small intestine is a very muscular tube. These muscles in the walls of the small intestine continue the process of peristalsis. They squeeze the mass of digesting

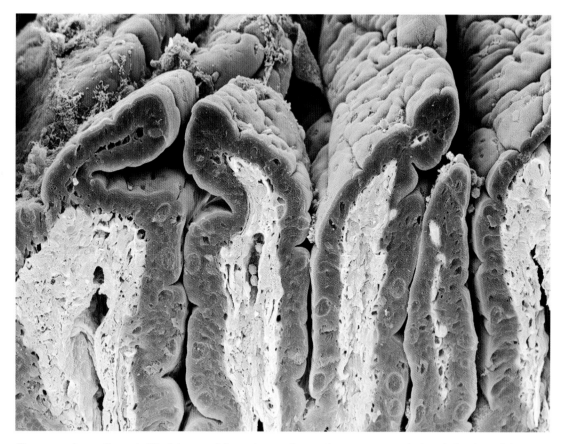

The muscular walls and villi of the small intestine work together to move and absorb food particles (light pink).

WHAT MAKES YOUR STOMACH GROWL?

Have you ever wondered what causes that rumbling sound you sometimes hear coming from inside your body? Stomach growling has fascinated people for thousands of years. The ancient Greeks actually named the condition *borborygmi,* which translates as "rumbling." The sound that can be heard outside the body comes from the squeezing and stretching of the walls of your digestive system. That growling comes from the stomach, but it is not the only noisy organ. The sound could also be coming from the small intestines. The muscle contractions of the stomach and intestinal walls also produce vibrations and the rumbling noise. You may think that your stomach only growls when it is empty and you are hungry, but it can occur at any time and it does not matter if the stomach is empty or full. It is usually louder when the stomach and intestines are empty because there is no food and liquid inside to block the noise.

food and push it along to the next section of intestine. Along the way, these contractions also mix the contents of the small intestine. This helps to break down the food and promotes better absorption. This process happens again and again until the food has been pushed all the way to the large intestine. In the large intestine, the contractions continue. Water is absorbed and the waste becomes more solid in the large intestine as the food finishes its journey through the digestive system.

Movement in the large intestine is generally slower than in the other digestive organs. However, the arrival of more food in the stomach activates more powerful contractions to push new feces into the sigmoid colon. This in turn pushes older feces stored in the sigmoid colon into the rectum. When the feces arrive in the rectum, the walls stretch. This sends a signal to the brain that the body needs to release the solid waste. When it is time, the muscles of the rectal wall contract to send the feces into the anal canal and out through the anus.

Moving in One Direction

The different sections of the gastrointestinal tract are separated from each other by special muscles called sphincters. When these muscles are closed tightly, they prevent food from moving between organs. Sphincters also regulate the movement of digested material through the system. There is a sphincter at the connection between the esophagus and stomach. This ring-shaped muscle controls the opening and passing of material between the two organs. As food coming down the esophagus approaches the closed sphincter, the surrounding muscles relax and allow the food to pass into the stomach. When this sphincter muscle is functioning properly it will not let the food travel back up from the stomach to the esophagus.

Similarly, there is a sphincter that divides the stomach from the small intestine. This muscle is called the pyloric sphincter, and it has a very important role. It regulates the flow of the semi-liquid food paste leaving the stomach. Pressure caused by the food in the stomach against the pyloric sphincter causes it to open slightly, allowing a small amount of food into the small intestine. Defecation is also controlled by two sphincter muscles that keep the anus closed tightly until the proper time.

PRODUCTION OF DIGESTIVE JUICES

Digestive juices play an important part in the digestive process. They come from different sources and work through various chemical and biological processes. The salivary glands in the mouth contribute the first type of digestive juice—saliva. Saliva contains amylase, which is an enzyme that breaks down starch.

Stomach acid is the next digestive juice to be added to the process. Glands in the stomach lining produce hydrochloric acid. They also secrete pepsin, an enzyme that digests protein. As the partially digested food reaches the small intestine, it already contains saliva, mucus, and gastric juices from the mouth, esophagus, and stomach. Juices from the liver and pancreas mix with juices from the small intestine in order to continue digestion in the intestines. Pancreatic juice contains many different enzymes that break down carbohydrates, fat, and proteins in food. The liver produces bile, which is stored in the gallbladder. When food enters the system, bile

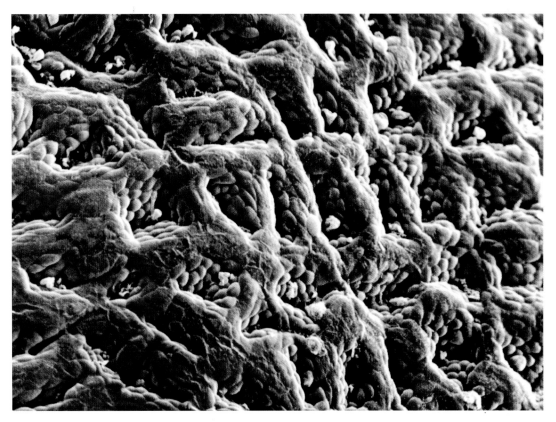

Gastric pits on the surface of the stomach help to increase the amount of area that is exposed to food. A larger surface area allows digestive organs to absorb more food.

SOURCE OF DIGESTIVE FLUID	DIGESTIVE FLUID SECRETION PER DAY
Salivary glands	1.5 pints (.71 liters)
Stomach acid	2 to 3 pints (.95 to 1.4 l)
Pancreatic juice	3 pints (1.4 l)
Bile	1.75 pints (.82 l)
Small intestine	2 to 3 pints (.95 to 1.4 l)

is squeezed out of the gallbladder into the bile ducts to reach the intestine. Other digestive enzymes and juices come directly from glands in the wall of the small intestine.

ABSORBING NUTRIENTS

The majority of nutrients absorbed during digestion are taken up by cells of the small intestine. Absorbed nutrients cross the mucosa and are carried through the bloodstream to other parts of the body—usually the liver—for storage or further chemical change. Before nutrients can be absorbed, however, they must be unlocked from the food and turned into a form that can be used by our bodies. The chemical process varies somewhat for different kinds of nutrients, and the action is carried out by different enzymes.

Amazing Enzymes

The chemical processes that happen every second in every cell of your body would not happen without enzymes. Enzymes are specialized proteins that speed up chemical reactions. They have many special properties.

One feature is that although they help change molecules and substances into different forms, they are not changed during the process. That way they are able to carry out their specific job over and over again. Digestive enzymes are secreted into the open, hollow space inside the organs. They are secreted by the salivary glands, stomach, pancreas, and small intestine. Each different enzyme performs one task. Without digestive enzymes, food would just move through the alimentary canal and the nutrients would not be taken out and absorbed by the body.

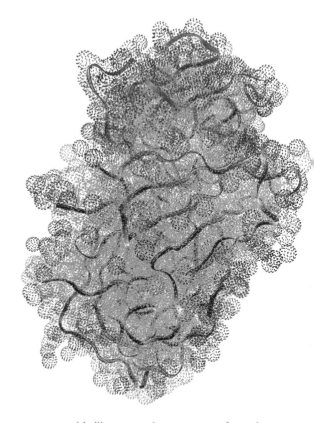

A computer graphic illustrates the structure of pepsin, an important protein-digesting enzyme.

Protein

Protein can be found in many types of foods, especially in meat, eggs, and beans. They are made up of small molecules called amino acids. Digestion breaks apart the proteins so that the body can use the amino acids as material to make new proteins and enzymes. Amino acids are essential for cell growth and repair. The digestion of proteins starts in the stomach and continues in the small intestine. Several enzymes from the stomach, small intestine, and pancreatic juices are responsible for breaking down proteins. Proteins can be very large molecules made up of many hundreds of amino acids. Enzymes break the large proteins down into smaller pieces made up of only a handful of amino acids. These smaller chains are called peptides. There are many sizes of small peptides that are produced by different stages of digestion. Eventually, the single amino acids are freed from the food. The amino acids can then be absorbed and reused.

ENZYME	PRODUCED BY	BREAKS DOWN
Amylase	salivary glands	starch
Carboxypeptidase	pancreas	protein
Chymotrypsin	pancreas	protein
Lactase	small intestine	lactose (complex sugar)
Lipase	pancreas	triglycerides (fat)
Maltase	small intestine	maltose (complex sugar)
Nuclease	pancreas	nucleic acids (DNA, RNA)
Pepsin	stomach	protein
Peptidase	small intestine	protein peptides
Sucrase	small intestine	sucrose (complex sugar)
Trypsin	pancreas	protein

Carbohydrates

Carbohydrates are an important source of energy for the body. Bread, potatoes, rice, fruits, and vegetables are common sources of carbohydrates. Simple sugars, such as glucose, are carbohydrates that can be used directly as energy. Complex carbohydrates, such as starch, are made up of chains of sugar molecules. These chains need to be broken down before the body can use them. During digestion, complex carbohydrates are processed into smaller units and eventually turned into simple sugars that provide energy. This is done by enzymes produced by the salivary glands, pancreas, and small intestine. For example, starch is digested in two steps. First, an enzyme in the saliva and pancreatic juice breaks the starch into molecules called maltose. Then an enzyme in the lining of the small intestine (maltase) splits the maltose into glucose molecules that can be absorbed into the blood. Glucose is carried through the bloodstream to the liver, where it is stored or used to provide energy for the body.

Fats

Fat is also an important source of energy for the body. The first step in digesting fat is to dissolve it into the watery liquid inside the intestines. Bile produced by the liver contains substances called bile acids. These acids force the fat to dissolve in water, which it will not do naturally. Once this happens, enzymes are able to break the large fat molecules into smaller molecules. These small molecules—including cholesterol and fatty acids—are absorbed and carried through the blood to be reassembled and stored as fat in different parts of the body. The molecules can also be used directly as energy. While having too much fat is bad for overall health, you need some fat in your diet and in your body. Fat helps insulate the body to keep a constant, warm internal temperature. It also surrounds internal organs and acts as a cushioning protective layer. While having too much cholesterol in the blood is bad and can cause diseases of the heart and

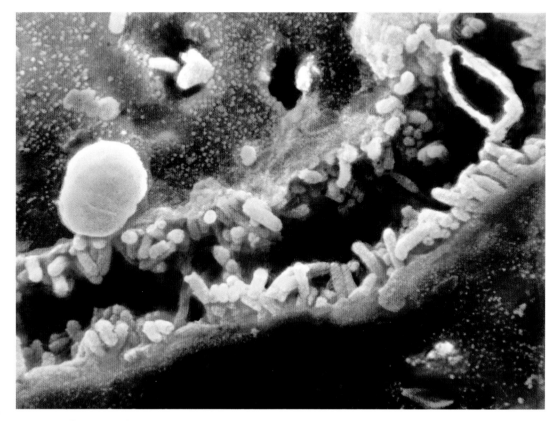

A liver cell (red-brown) secretes bile, which travels to the gallbladder through tiny ducts called bile canaliculi (green).

blood vessels, you need some cholesterol because it is used to make cell membranes for all the body's cells.

Vitamins, Minerals, and Fiber

Other important parts of food that are absorbed from the small intestine are vitamins and minerals, which are used in many processes in the body. Vitamins A, B, and C are all absorbed by the intestines. Minerals such as calcium, sodium, iron, zinc, and many others also come from the foods we eat and are essential for many functions in the body.

Fiber is a material from plants that cannot be digested and no nutrients are absorbed from it. It passes through the digestive system untouched and is a major component of feces.

CONTROLLING THE DIGESTIVE PROCESS

The entire digestive system, including the movement of muscles in the digestive organ walls and the secretion of digestive juices, is controlled by nerves of the autonomic nervous system and by hormones. The only part of digestion that you can actively control is what type of food you eat, how much you eat, and how many times you chew your food before swallowing. Once the partially chewed up food reaches the back of the mouth and triggers the swallowing reflex, the rest of the digestive process happens without you having to make any other decisions. Putting food in the mouth triggers many hormones and processes like production of saliva and gastric juices. The same process begins when we see, smell, or think about eating food. Also, food in the stomach triggers hormones to turn on the secretion of acid and to release digestive enzymes.

Hormone Regulators

The major hormones that control the functions of the digestive system are produced and released by cells in the mucosa of the stomach and small intestine. Before they can cause any effects, however, they must first be released into the blood, travel back to the heart, and then return to the digestive system. Then they can stimulate the production and release of digestive juices and cause the muscle contractions that grind and transport food.

Do you start to drool when you smell delicious food? Saliva production can be a sign that your body is getting ready to digest food.

There are several hormones involved in controlling digestion. One is gastrin, which causes the stomach to produce hydrocholoric acid for dissolving food. Gastrin also assists in the normal growth of the mucosal layer lining the stomach, small intestine, and colon. Another hormone called secretin causes the pancreas to send out its digestive juice, stimulates the stomach to produce the protein-digesting enzyme pepsin, and also makes the liver produce bile. The hormone cholecystokinin causes the pancreas to grow and to produce the enzymes of pancreatic juice, and it also causes the gallbladder to empty the stored bile into the small intestine.

Other hormones affect appetite, such as ghrelin that makes the body feel hungry. Peptide YY is a hormone that makes the body feel full. Both of these hormones have effects on the brain to help regulate the how much food we eat in order to gain energy.

Nerve Regulators

Several nerves help to control the action of the digestive system. Some nerves connect the digestive organs to the brain or spinal cord. These nerves deliver chemical messages that cause the muscles of the digestive organs to squeeze harder in order to force the food through the digestive tract. These nerve signals can also tell the stomach and pancreas to produce more digestive juices. For example, the vagus nerve runs from the brain to the stomach. It sends messages to the cells of the stomach lining to secrete stomach acid in response to the smell or taste of food. There are also nerves that are located within the walls of the esophagus, stomach, small intestine, and colon. These nerves are triggered to act when the walls of the hollow organs are stretched by food. They send messages throughout the digestive system in order to speed up or slow down the production of juices or movement of food.

All of these process and parts work together to move and digest food. When certain parts do not work, problems arise.

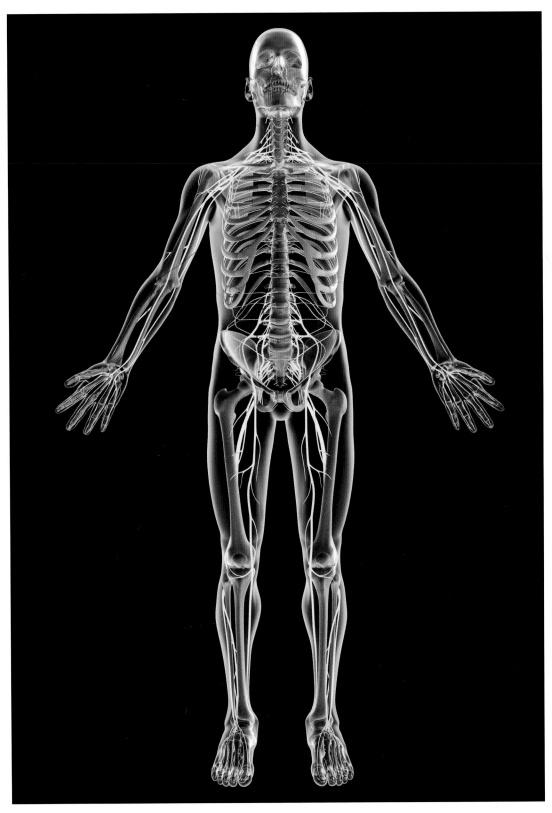

The nervous system is made up the brain, the spinal cord, and a complex network of nerves found throughout the body.

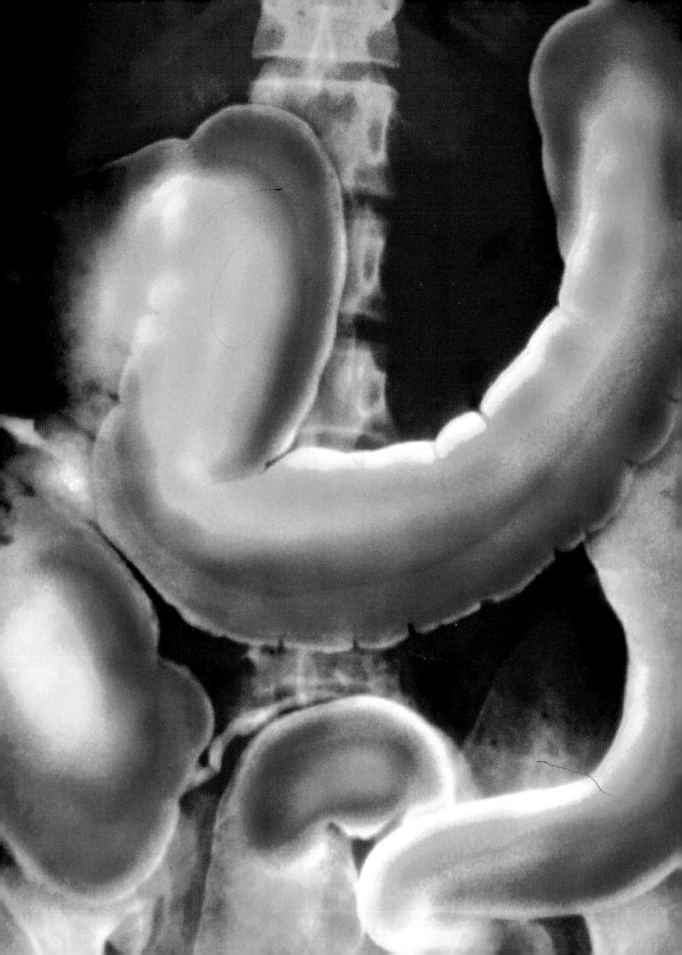

Digestive Diseases and Conditions

here are many different types of digestive disorders. Digestive disorders can affect various organs in the digestive system, and have different symptoms, causes, and treatments. Some common problems include indigestion, vomiting, nausea, and diarrhea. These can be the result of eating too much, eating food that has spoiled or has bacteria in it, or having an illness like the flu. Unless a person has very serious symptoms or the problem lasts for many days, it is usually unnecessary to see a doctor because these types of digestive problems normally will go away on their own. Other disorders can be more serious and may require medical attention. Doctors who specialize in treating problems with

Doctors can use X rays to look at digestive organs and diagnose, or determine, digestive problems.

the digestive system are called gastroenterologists. A gastroenterologist can diagnose digestive problems through examination and by performing special tests. Based on the results, the gastroenterologist may prescribe certain medications to treat the problem.

COMMON SYMPTOMS

There are several common digestive problems that everyone has at some point in their lives. Nausea, vomiting, diarrhea, constipation, bloating, and gas are some examples. These problems are often symptoms of indigestion, which is basically a disruption in the digestive process. However, sometimes these symptoms are a sign of illness or imbalances in the body.

Nausea and Vomiting

Nausea is the sensation of having to vomit, or throw up. Nausea can be caused by irritation in the digestive tract, but it can also be caused by things not related to digestion. For example, people who get motion sickness or bad headaches from pain, strong smells, or bright lights will usually experience nausea. Stress or other strong emotions can also cause nausea. Nausea is usually triggered by your brain and nerves sending and receiving signals from your digestive organs. Sometimes nausea leads to vomiting, but not always. Treatment for nausea may include lying down, resting, or taking certain medications.

Vomiting occurs when food—undigested or partially digested—travels back up through the digestive tract and out your mouth. The muscles of your digestive organs contract and move the food back up the way it first came down. You may vomit if you have eaten spoiled food—which irritates your stomach or parts of your intestines. Certain infections from bacteria, viruses, or other microorganisms can also cause vomiting. Eating too much is also a cause for vomiting. The stomach cannot handle too much food, so your body expels it by vomiting. In many cases, vomiting will

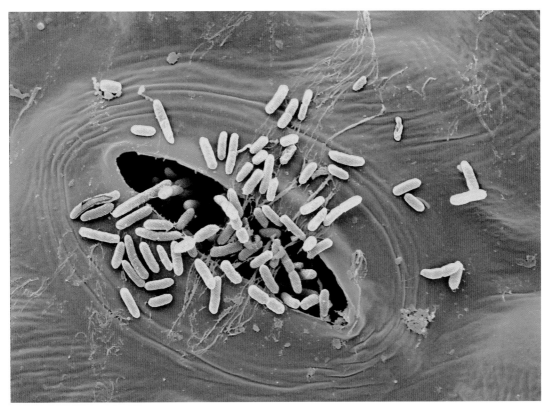

Escherichia coli *(also known as* E. coli*) bacteria can be found on the surface of food that has not been cleaned or cooked properly. If someone eats this unwashed piece of lettuce, the* E. coli *(orange) will most likely cause vomiting, diarrhea, and other digestive problems.*

stop when the irritation goes away. Constant vomiting, however, can lead to dehydration or other serious problems. A person experiencing frequent, very painful, or bloody vomiting should be examined by a doctor.

Diarrhea

Diarrhea is a common condition that is also a symptom of other disorders. It is described as having frequent, loose, or watery feces, and a feeling sense of having to defecate urgently and often. Eating spoiled food, having a viral infection, or suffering from other illnesses may cause diarrhea. Whatever the cause, the process that causes diarrhea is usually the same. In diarrhea, the amount of time food residues remain in the large intestine is reduced. This means that there is not enough time for water to be reabsorbed. That is why the stools are not solid and can be very watery. It can be associated with abdominal cramps or pain. Usually diarrhea runs its course and your digestive system goes back to normal. However, some medications can be used to harden stool and relieve the cramping.

Constipation

Constipation is—in some ways—the opposite of diarrhea. It is described as defecating fewer than three times per week, passing unusually hard stools, and sometimes having difficulty with bowel movements. Sometimes people who are constipated have a constant feeling of needing to go but are unable to do so. Constipation may be caused by a lack of fiber or too little fluid in the diet. It may also be the result of emotional or physical stress. Some medications people take for other conditions can also cause constipation. Usually, constipation will end in a few days, but there are medications and fiber supplements that soften the feces. Eating certain foods can also help make bowel movements easier.

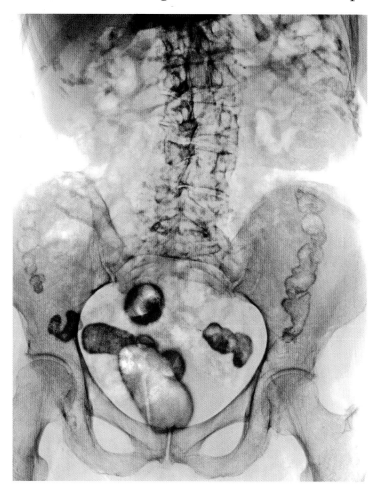

This woman is suffering from severe constipation. A colored X ray shows the hardened stools (pink and orange) that are stuck in the intestines.

Bloating and Gas

When a person is bloated, his or her stomach usually feels tight and full. Bloating often occurs after large meals, but it can also be a sign of different digestive disorders. Gas—or a lot of air in the digestive organs—is what causes the bloated feeling. This gas build-up comes from swallowing air. Intestinal gas naturally builds up as you digest food. Food that does not get digested properly can also cause gas as bacteria feed on the food and release gas.

Gas that builds up in the stomach is often released as burps that come out of your mouth. Intestinal gas is called flatus. Releasing this gas through the anus is called flatulence, or, more commonly, farting. Flatus that is released usually has an unpleasant smell. The smell comes from a combination of the different gases—such

Stomach pain can be a symptom of many different digestive problems.

as hydrogen, methane, carbon dioxide, and ammonia—that mix together inside the intestines. Though it can sometimes be embarrassing and unpleasant, passing gas is a normal body process.

GASTROESOPHAGEAL REFLUX DISEASE

The most common disorder that occurs in the esophagus is called gastroesophageal reflux disease, or GERD for short. Sometimes people refer to this condition as heartburn, but it has nothing to do with the heart. Actually, heartburn is caused by acid from the stomach flowing in

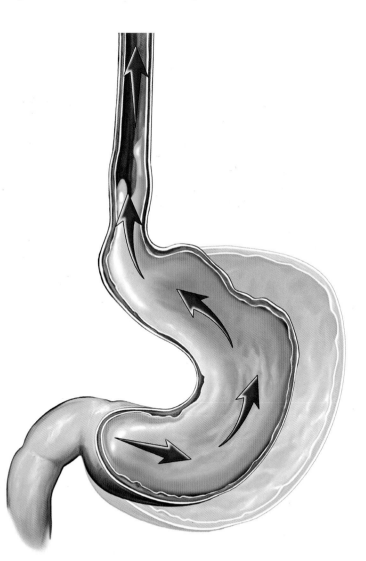

In GERD, which is sometimes called acid reflux, acid (yellow) travels from the stomach up to the esophagus, where it causes pain. Severe or constant GERD usually results in damage to the esophagus. Fortunately, doctors can recommend a variety of treatments for GERD.

the wrong direction back into the esophagus. GERD happens when the sphincter muscle that separates the esophagus from the stomach is not working properly. It should only allow food and digestive juices to pass in one direction—from the esophagus to the stomach. The backflow of acid is called reflux. The stomach acid irritates the lining of the esophagus and makes people feel a burning pain in their chest. This feeling can affect the upper middle part of the chest and up into the neck and throat. Some people with reflux problems can taste the sour acid in the back of their throat. These feelings of burning and pressure usually happen after eating and can last for hours.

There are several types of treatment for heartburn. Avoiding certain foods, such as chocolate, coffee, greasy or spicy food, and alcohol can help because these foods tend to increase acid production. People with heartburn who smoke should stop smoking because tobacco makes the stomach produce more acid. Tobacco can also cause the sphincter muscle to relax and allow acid to move back up the esophagus. Losing weight if someone is overweight and avoiding bedtime snacks are also strategies for controlling heartburn. Not lying down right after eating can also help. However, sometimes only medication will help. There are medications called antacids that balance the digestive acid. Other types of drugs block the production of acid in the stomach and help decrease the symptoms of GERD.

PANCREATITIS

Pancreatitis is a rare disease that causes the damage and inflammation to the pancreas. This happens when digestive enzymes produced by the pancreas start attacking the pancreas itself instead of the food in the small intestine. Patients with pancreatitis feel very sick and often have nausea, vomiting, fever, and increased pulse rate. The condition usually starts with a pain in the upper abdomen that lasts for a few days. The pain may be severe and constant, and may be located just in the abdomen or felt in the back and other areas.

There are two forms of pancreatitis called acute and chronic. Acute pancreatitis happens suddenly and may be severe with many complications. It may be life-threatening, but most patients are able to recover fully. Acute pancreatitis is diagnosed by a blood test that shows high levels of digestive enzymes in the blood. Treatment is usually done in the hospital, where the patient will receive intravenous fluids and nutrition.

If a patient with acute pancreatitis is not treated or continues to cause damage to the pancreas, that person may suffer from chronic pancreatitis, in which the symptoms continue. Chronic pancreatitis can be extremely painful and the damage to the pancreas causes it to malfunction. This can lead to weight loss, diabetes (a disorder related to blood sugar levels), and may affect digestion. Chronic pancreatitis can be the result of long-term alcohol abuse, or it could develop after only one attack of acute pacreatitis if the pancreas is severely damaged. Laboratory tests and imaging tools can help diagnose chronic pancreatitis, and it is managed by pain relievers, medication that contains pancreatic enzymes, and reducing the amount of fat in the diet.

DIVERTICULOSIS AND DIVERTICULITIS

When solid waste becomes very hard, the colon has to put more effort into pushing the stools along. If this happens frequently, it can cause the wall of the colon to stick out like a pouch because of the extra pressure it has been going through. These pouches are called diverticula, and the condition is known as diverticulosis. Sometimes these pouches can become infected and cause pain and fever—a condition called diverticulitis. If one of the pouches rupture, the infection could spread to the whole abdomen

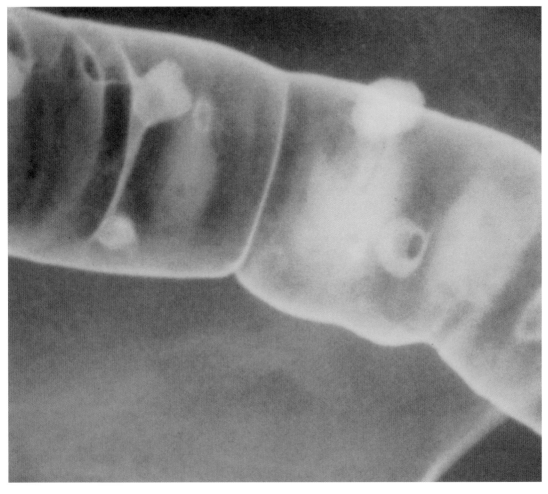

An X ray shows the small pouches that have developed on the walls of the colon affected by diverticulosis. Diverticulitis occurs when these pouches become infected.

and affect other organs. The symptoms of diverticulitis include pain in left lower abdomen, fever, and a sudden change in bowel movements.

Doctors can perform several tests to diagnose diverticulitis. They may look inside the colon with examinations like a sigmoidoscopy or colonoscopy, in which a camera is inserted into the rectum and up through parts of the intestines. Treatment options include surgery to remove the part of the colon that has the pouches, increasing the amount of fiber and liquid in the diet, pain medication, and medication to control infection.

DIAGNOSTIC TESTS

Gastroenterologists often order special tests to help diagnose diseases of the gastrointestinal tract when patients have abdominal pain, nausea, vomiting, heartburn, diarrhea, constipation, blood in the feces, or unexplained weight loss.

Abdominal X ray

An abdominal X ray can show a blockage, tear, or other physical problem of the intestinal tract. An X ray is a picture that uses waves of energy (radiation) instead of light to take a picture of what is inside your body. Organs absorb different amounts of the radiation and this is seen on the X ray as varying degrees of black, white, or gray.

Barium studies

Barium is a thick, white chalky substance that is used in several diagnostic tests for problems with the digestive system. Barium shows up on X ray images and helps show details of the inside of the intestines and other organs. A barium esophagram, also called a barium swallow, may be ordered for patients with difficult or painful swallowing, coughing, choking, a sensation of something stuck in the throat, or chest pain. The test is performed when a patient drinks a liquid that contains barium and is then X rayed. Another test involving barium is called a barium enema. It also requires the use of barium but in a different manner. A small tube is inserted in the rectum and a liquid containing barium is injected into the large intestine. The barium spreads throughout the colon. X ray images are taken and doctors can see the structure of the large intestine.

Endoscopy

An upper endoscopy involves insertion of a thin flexible tube through the mouth to allow the doctor to look inside the esophagus, stomach, and first part of the small intestine. This test may be ordered for a patient who is having difficulty swallowing, nausea, vomiting, acid reflux, bleeding, indigestion, abdominal pain, or chest pain. The thin, flexible, lighted tube called an endoscope transmits an image to a computer screen so that the gastroenterologist can carefully examine the lining of the organs.

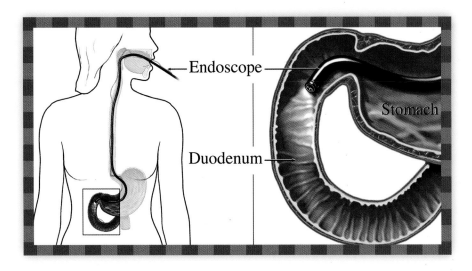

Endoscope

Stomach

Duodenum

The endoscope can also blow air into the stomach to expand the folds of tissue and make it easier for the physician to examine the stomach. Abnormalities such as inflammation or bleeding that do not show up well on X rays can be observed through the endoscope.

Sigmoidoscopy and Colonoscopy

Both of these tests allow the doctor to check for inflammation and bleeding inside the large intestine. Doctors use a thin, flexible, lighted instrument that looks like a long tube that is connected to a computer and screen. The end of the instrument, either a sigmoidoscope or colonoscope, is inserted into a patients rectum to view the inside of the rectum and colon. A sigmoidoscopy can be used to see the last

2 feet (61 cm) of the colon. However, the entire colon and rectum can be observed by performing a colonoscopy. It can show if there are any abnormal growths in the colon, bleeding, or other problems. Sometimes small growths can be removed during colonoscopies.

Virtual colonoscopies use X rays and scanning equipment instead of an inserted scope. However, virtual colonoscopies are still being fine-tuned, and if abnormal growths are found, a traditional colonoscopy would still be needed.

New diagnostic technologies are constantly being developed. This is good because better technology means faster diagnosis and more effective treatment.

INFLAMMATORY BOWEL DISEASE

Crohn's disease and ulcerative colitis are the two most common inflammatory bowel diseases. Both cause inflammation in the intestines and have similar symptoms including abdominal pain and bloody diarrhea. Patients may also feel tired, lose weight, not feel hungry, have a fever, or be dehydrated. While Crohn's disease and ulcerative colitis are both inflammatory bowel diseases and have many similarities, there are also important differences between the two diseases. Crohn's disease can

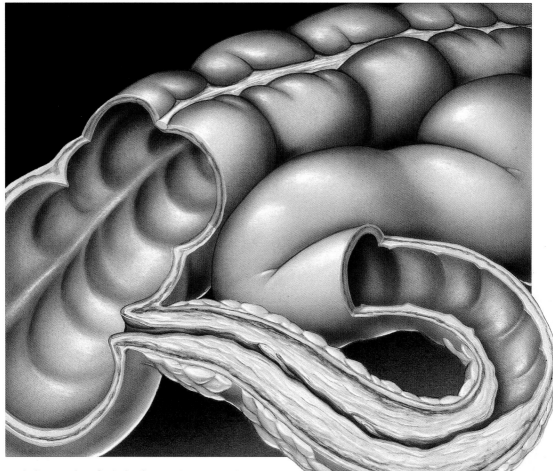

In this illustration, Crohn's disease has caused inflammation in the ileum, the lowest part of the small intestine.

affect any part of the gastrointestinal system from the mouth to the anus, while ulcerative colitis only affects the colon. Usually, however, Crohn's disease affects the colon and the ileum, which is the last part of the small intestine. Crohn's disease has inflammation affecting the entire wall of the intestine, while ulcerative colitis only affects the innermost layer. The inflammation caused by Crohn's disease can cause intestinal swelling, scarring, and block the flow of digested food. It can also cause a sore in the inflamed area called a fistula, which can bleed or become infected. A fistula is an abnormal connection between two organs or between an organ and the skin.

The cause of these diseases is unknown. To diagnose Crohn's disease or ulcerative colitis a doctor may need to do a colonoscopy. People with Crohn's disease and ulcerative colitis often go for long periods, even years, with no symptoms. However, the disease usually comes back at some point. Treatment may include medication, surgery, nutritional supplements, or a combination of these therapies.

IRRITABLE BOWEL SYNDROME

The disorder called irritable bowel syndrome (IBS) is a common problem. Symptoms include bloating, gas, temporary abdominal pain and cramps, constipation, and diarrhea. Some people have both constipation and diarrhea, just at different times. Many people have IBS, but a person who has blood in the feces, weight loss, fever, or continuous pain should see a doctor because these are not symptoms of IBS and could be signs of a more serious disease.

In IBS, the large intestine is affected and does not work properly. The exact cause, however, is unknown. Treatment includes reducing stress, changing the food a person eats, eating smaller meals, and also eating more fiber. There are also medications that can help control IBS symptoms.

ULCERS

Ulcers are sores that are most often found in the stomach and the first part of the small intestine. Symptoms of ulcers are a burning pain in the abdomen, nausea, vomiting, loss of appetite, or weight loss. Upper abdominal pain is the major symptom, and it usually occurs between meals

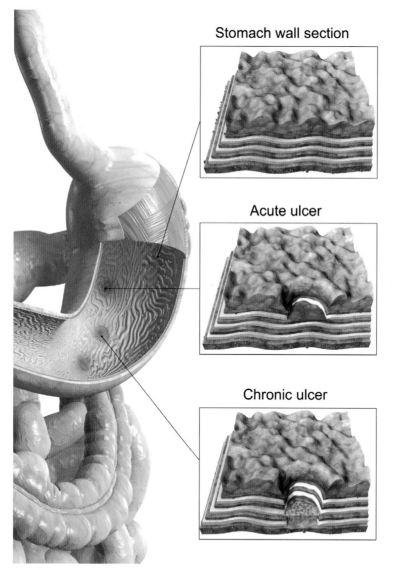

Stomach wall section

Acute ulcer

Chronic ulcer

Stomach tissue damaged by an acute ulcer (middle) usually heals with time and medical treatment. Chronic ulcers (bottom) affect more layers of stomach tissue and muscle. These types of ulcers take a longer time to heal and sometimes involve scarring of the stomach lining.

and can last from minutes to hours. In the past, doctors thought that ulcers were caused by stressful situations in a person's life. However, now doctors know that ulcers are caused by bacteria called *Helicobacter pylori*, or *H. pylori*. Ulcers may also be caused by taking a specific class of medication called nonsteroidal anti-inflammatory drugs (NSAIDs). These drugs are given for the treatment of pain, but can also weaken the mucosal lining so that the acid in digestive juices harms the organ and causes bleeding. NSAIDs should be avoided by patients who develop an ulcer.

Ulcers caused by bacteria can be treated successfully with antibiotics. Also, medications that reduce acid can also help relieve symptoms. Most ulcers can be healed with medication, but some may require surgery to correct.

HEMORRHOIDS

Hemorrhoids are caused by groups of swollen veins in the lower rectum or at the anus. Symptoms include bleeding in the rectum, pain, and itching. Treatments for hemorrhoids include increasing fiber and fluid intake and taking a fiber supplement. There are also creams that can control the pain and itching that can be applied to the affected area. Serious hemorrhoid cases may require surgery.

COLORECTAL CANCER

Although cancer can affect any of the digestive organs, the most common location is the large intestine. This type of cancer is called colorectal cancer because it specifically affects the colon and rectum. Colorectal cancer is the third most common cause of cancer-related death in the United States in both men and women.

The most common symptom of colorectal cancer is rectal bleeding. Most cases of colorectal cancer start with wart-like growths on the inner lining of the colon or rectum. These growths are called polyps, but not all

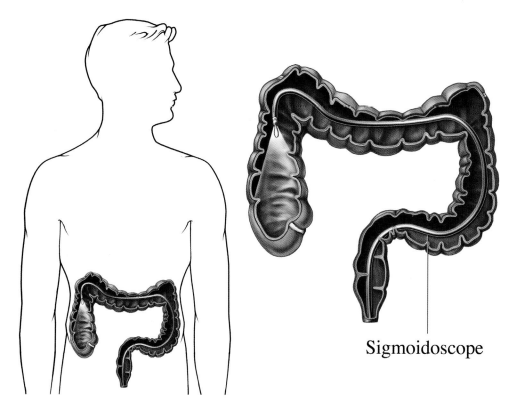

Sigmoidoscope

Most doctors recommend sigmoidoscopies and colonoscopies for men and women who are fifty years old or older and for others who are likely to develop colorectal cancer. It is important to detect and treat cancer in its early stages.

polyps have the potential to turn into cancer. Some do become cancerous, but these polyps can be found on routine colonoscopy exams. These exams look for cancer or polyps and can find them before a person has any symptoms. The polyps can be removed and this increases the chance that the person will live and not develop colorectal cancer. Doctors recommend that everyone age fifty and older have a colonoscopy checkup every ten years. If someone has a family history of colorectal cancer or has already had polyps removed, they may also have an annual test to check for blood in the stool and a sigmoidoscopy every three to five years.

FOOD-RELATED DISORDERS

Food Allergies

Doctors estimate that approximately 12 million Americans suffer from food allergies. An allergy is an immune system response to something safe that the body mistakenly believes is harmful. In the case of food allergies, a certain food is the substance that the body is trying to protect itself from. People can be allergic to any type of food, but some common foods that account for the majority of all food allergies are milk, eggs, peanuts, nuts (from trees, such as walnuts), fish, shellfish (such as shrimp), soy, and wheat.

It is important to carefully read labels on packaged foods if you have a food allergy.

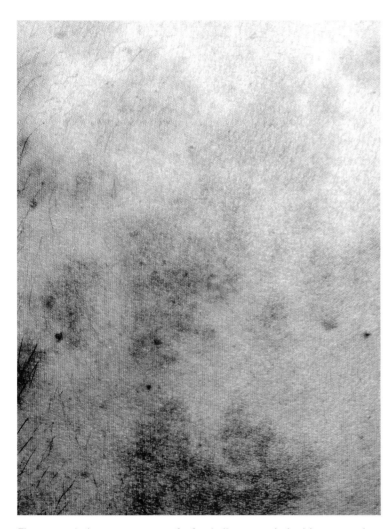

The most obvious symptoms of a food allergy are itchy hives or rashes that develop on the skin. However, some food allergies cause digestive problems like diarrhea or vomiting.

A person with a food allergy has a negative response when he or she eats that particular food—sometimes even just a very small amount of that food. When someone with a food allergy eats that particular trigger food, the immune system releases massive amounts of chemicals to protect the body. This is known as an allergic reaction. The reaction can happen immediately or a few hours after coming into contact with the food. An allergic reaction can be mild with symptoms like itchy rashes on the skin or swelling. Some of the first signs of an allergic reaction to food are having a runny nose, developing itchy skin rashes, tingling of the mouth, tongue, or lips, coughing, or wheezing. Other people may feel strong effects in their digestive system, such as stomach pain, nausea, diarrhea, or vomiting. Sometimes food allergies can cause severe reactions that can affect the heart, and lungs, and may potentially be deadly. When the reaction is sudden and severe, it is known as anaphylaxis. A person's tongue may swell up, they may have difficulty breathing, and their blood pressure might drop.

To find out if someone has a food allergy, they can have special tests done by a doctor to find out exactly what kind of food makes them sick. People at risk for the most severe reactions need to be very careful about avoiding the food they are allergic to, and may need to carry special instructions and medications just in case they accidentally eat the food and have a medical emergency. Sometimes, food allergies will disappear as a person gets older.

Celiac Disease

Celiac disease is a chronic digestive disease in which patients have difficulty absorbing nutrients from the food they eat. This is usually due to inflammation or irritation in the small intestine. Celiac disease is caused by a certain protein found in foods like wheat, barley, rye and related grains, called gluten, that some people are sensitive to. Celiac disease is similar to a food allergy because the immune system reacts against the gluten protein and causes an inflammatory reaction in the walls of the small intestine. This reaction damages the villi lining the small intestine and decreases the body's ability to absorb food. The intestine begins to heal if gluten is removed from the diet because this reduces inflammation.

People with celiac disease can have very different symptoms. Some of the most common symptoms include abdominal pain, bloating, diarrhea, and weight loss, but people may also feel weak or tired, have low levels of certain vitamins and minerals, or have pain in their joints. Tests for celiac disease include blood tests and endoscopy. Celiac disease is treated by avoiding all foods that contain gluten. Foods that contain gluten and are not allowed in any form include wheat, rye, and barley. There are obvious foods to avoid, such as breads, crackers, and cereals, but these ingredients may also be found on some foods, broths, croutons, pastas, marinades, processed meats, and sauces. Patients with celiac disease need to stay on a gluten-free diet for the rest of their lives. While this may be difficult at first, patients usually get used to it and the benefits of not having symptoms greatly outweigh the inconvenience of reading food labels and avoiding certain foods.

LACTOSE INTOLERANCE

People who have lactose intolerance cannot digest foods with lactose in them. Lactose is the sugar found in milk and foods made with milk. Lactose intolerance is not a serious health problem, but it can make people uncomfortable after eating foods with lactose. They may feel nauseous, have diarrhea, abdominal cramps, or gas.

A person who is lactose intolerant must learn to read food labels carefully, and then avoid lactose-containing products. He or she should look out for ingredients that include cream, whey, curds, milk by-products, dried milk, milk solids, and powdered milk. If any of these words are listed on a label, the product contains lactose. Some stores sell lactose-reduced dairy products. In these products lactase—the

People who do not have enough lactase, the enzyme that digests milk sugars, need to watch out for any food with cheese, yogurt, cream, or milk.

enzyme that breaks down lactose—has been added to decrease the amount of lactose. There are also medications—in the form of pills or liquid—that contain lactase.

Whether a digestive problem is caused by the food a person eats or a medical condition, it is always a good idea to practice good digestive health. Good general health cannot be accomplished without taking care of your digestive system.

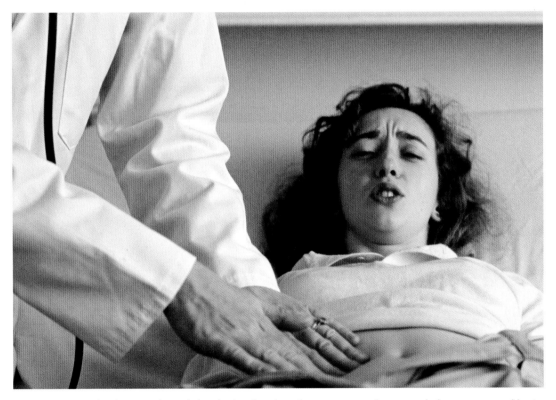

If you have very bad stomach or abdominal pains that do not seem to have an obvious cause and last a long time, you should see a doctor. Not only can the doctor help relieve the pain, but he or she can also diagnose digestive disorders before they become dangerous.

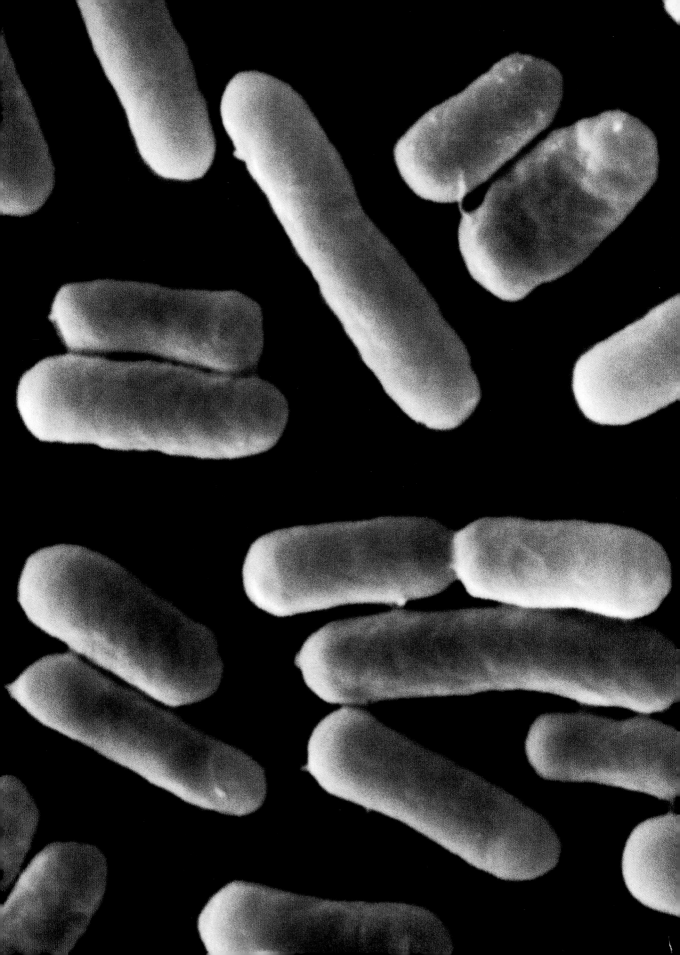

4

Maintaining a Healthy Digestive System

ood nutrition and a balanced diet are the best ways to keep the digestive system healthy and working properly. Eating too much processed food, sugars, and fats and not eating enough fiber, fruits, and vegetables can contribute to digestive problems. Eating too quickly can also be part of the problem. There are simple things that you can do every day to help your digestive system do its job.

Salmonella *bacteria on unwashed and uncooked food can cause problems for your digestive system. All food should be washed properly and meat should always be cooked to a safe temperature. Special thermometers can be used to determine how long to cook your meat.*

Your whole body needs water to function properly. Drinking enough water will also help you digest your food properly. Not drinking enough water can sometimes lead to constipation.

DRINK WATER

Most people do not drink enough water every day. Water is an essential part of digestion, but it is often forgotten. Water also plays an important role in many other processes for overall health. Most of our body is actually made of water. In fact, about 60 percent of body weight comes from water. Water is lost from the body through breath, sweat, urine, and feces and needs to constantly be replenished.

Not having enough water in the body causes dehydration. This happens when the body uses more water than it is taking in. By the time someone feels thirsty, it is possible to already be slightly dehydrated. That is why it is important to drink water throughout the day, even when you do not feel thirsty. Even being just a little dehydrated can decrease energy levels and make you tired. Common causes of dehydration include vomiting, diarrhea, excessive sweating, and strenuous activity. Signs that a person may be dehydrated are mild to excessive thirst, fatigue, headache, dry mouth, little or no urine production, muscle weakness, or dizziness. In cases of extreme dehydration, fluids may need to be delivered intravenously through a needle and tube directly into the bloodstream.

Everyone has different needs for how much water they should drink each day. Water intake depends on a person's level of physical activity, the climate of where he or she lives, and other factors. Doctors estimate that drinking about 8 cups (1.9 l) of water along with a normal diet will usually replace the lost fluids. If someone is very active and exercising a lot they will need more water, especially during and right after the activity. Hot or humid weather can make you sweat more and requires additional fluid intake. Also, women who are pregnant or breast-feeding need additional fluids to stay hydrated.

Drinking is not the only way to take in water and fluids. Fruits like watermelon are high in water content.

Drinking plain, ordinary water is an obvious way to make sure the body has enough water, but there are also other ways. Tea, coffee, juices, and soda all contain water, but they also may contain things that plain water does not, such as sugar, calories, and substances like caffeine. These types of drinks should not be a major portion of your daily total fluid intake. There is also water in food, which can add about 20 percent of the amount of water you need each day. For example, many fruits and vegetables are high in water content. Watermelon and cucumbers are nearly 100 percent water by weight. Beverages such as milk and juice are also mostly made up of water. Even caffeinated beverages, such as coffee, tea or soda, can contribute to the daily water requirement. However, too many caffeinated beverages can dehydrate you and cause other problems in your body.

It is also important to know that as you get older your body is less able to sense dehydration and send your brain signals of thirst. Excessive thirst and increased urination can be signs of a more serious medical condition. You should talk to your doctor if you experience either problem.

FIND FIBER

Fiber is found in many foods. Instead of being used for energy, fiber is excreted from our bodies and passes through the digestive system without being absorbed like other nutrients into the bloodstream. Fiber helps to move the mass of digested and undigested food through the intestines. It helps promote regular defecation and prevent constipation. So even if it does not work like other nutrients, it is important for healthy digestive processes. There are two types of fiber, insoluble and soluble, but they are both indigestible and are both important to have in the diet. The difference is that soluble fiber forms a gel when mixed with liquid, while insoluble fiber passes through the intestines without changing.

Many people eat bran cereals to help meet their daily fiber requirements. A doctor or nutritionist can help you determine what your daily fiber intake should be.

Research has shown that a high-fiber diet may improve or prevent chronic constipation, coronary heart disease, hemorrhoids, diverticulitis, cholesterol levels, irritable bowel syndrome, and colorectal cancer. The daily recommended intake is 20 to 35 grams (.71 to 1.2 ounces) per day. Studies have shown that Americans do not eat enough fiber, and that on average we eat only 10 to 15 grams per day. It is important to try to substitute high-fiber foods in place of high-fat and low-fiber foods whenever possible. Foods that are high in fiber include beans, potatoes, soybeans, chickpeas, pears, broccoli, apples, barley, oat bran, and brown rice.

EAT FRUITS AND VEGETABLES

A diet filled with many different fruits and vegetables is associated with decreased risk for many chronic diseases. The goal is to have four to five

Fruits and vegetables provide your body with nutrients like vitamins, minerals, and fiber.

servings of fruits and vegetables every day. They are natural sources of many vitamins, minerals, and fiber. Most fruits and vegetables also have relatively few calories relative to their volume, which makes you feel full after eating fewer calories. This can help with weight loss and weight management. Fruits such as apricots, bananas, dates, grapes, oranges, grapefruit, mangoes, melons, peaches, pineapples, strawberries, tangerines, and tomatoes, are a rich source of potassium, magnesium, and fiber. So are vegetables such as potatoes, carrots, green peas, squash, broccoli, turnip greens, collards, kale, spinach, artichokes, green beans, lima beans, and sweet potatoes.

CHOOSE WHOLE GRAINS

An average balanced diet includes six to eight servings of grain per day. While all grains provide a source of energy and fiber, it is best to choose whole grains when possible. Products made with whole grains, have more nutrients and fiber than other refined grains. Whole-grain foods include whole wheat and multigrain breads, cereals, and crackers, brown or wild rice, and whole wheat pasta. Refined-grain foods, such as white rice and white bread do not have as much fiber or nutrients. They can also increase the amount of sugar you are taking in.

LIMIT FAT

By avoiding deep-fried foods and choosing healthier cooking methods, such as broiling, grilling, roasting, and steaming, you can limit the amount

Too much fried or oily food can clog your blood vessels and affect your weight. These kinds of food can also cause stomach upset, such as diarrhea, bloating, and gas.

of fat in your diet. The daily recommended allowance for an average diet is about two to three servings of fats. When cooking with fats, olive oil is a healthy choice because it contains monounsaturated fat. This type of fat can lower the risk of heart disease by reducing levels of bad cholesterol in your blood. Unlike olive oil, fats such as butter contain saturated and trans fats, which increase your risk of heart disease by increasing cholesterol levels. It is better to substitute olive oil for saturated fats in the diet, rather than adding more olive oil to the diet.

CHOOSE LEAN SOURCES OF PROTEIN

Lean meats, poultry, fish, eggs, beans, lentils, nuts, seeds, tofu, and low-fat dairy products are all good choices of protein. These foods are rich sources of protein and magnesium. It is recommended to include six or

Tofu—which is made from soybeans—can be served in many different ways. Some people even use tofu as a meat substitute.

fewer servings of lean protein daily. Nuts and seeds, such as sunflower and pumpkin seeds, are good choices for snacks because they are also sources of energy, magnesium, potassium, protein, and fiber.

Without your digestive system your body could not function properly. It helps you use important nutrients and move body wastes. Knowing how your digestive system works and what you can do to keep it healthy will help your overall health.

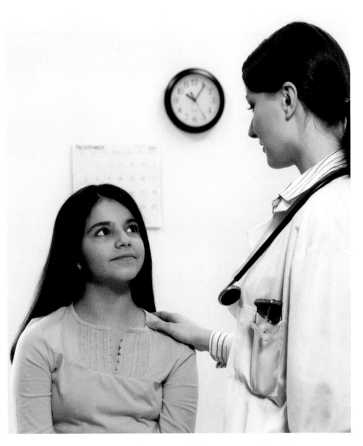

Regular visits with your doctor can help you stay healthy.

abdomen—The large cavity in the center of the body between the chest and the hips where most of the digestive organs are located.

absorption—The process in which food nutrients are taken from the food inside the intestines into the bloodstream for distribution to all cells in the body.

acute—Having a short and relatively severe course. Some health disorders are considered acute.

amino acids—The basic building blocks of proteins that are essential to life.

antacid—A medication that counteracts or neutralizes acids in the stomach or duodenum.

anus—The lower opening of the digestive tract through which feces (bowel movements) leave the body.

barium—The main ingredient of the testing solution given by mouth or rectum to patients undergoing certain digestive tests. Barium outlines the hollow organs of the digestive tract and makes them visible on X-ray images.

bile—A fluid produced by the liver and stored in the gallbladder that aids in the digestion of fats and is used by the body to dispose of wastes that do not dissolve in water.

bloating—A feeling of excessive fullness in the abdomen, often occurring after meals.

cholesterol—A chemical compound known as a lipid, which is a type of fat found in meats and produced in the body by the liver.

chronic—Lasting for a long time, often years. A disease or illness can be chronic if it lasts a long time or keeps coming back.

chyme—The thick liquid mixture of partly digested food and stomach juices that passes from the stomach into the intestines.

colon—The longest part of the large intestine that extends from the cecum to the rectum.

colonoscope—A long, flexible, narrow instrument passed through the anus to look into the colon.

constipation—Infrequent or difficult passage of feces.

defecation—The process of forcing feces out of the body through the anus. It is also called egestion, having a bowel movement, or pooping.

diarrhea—A condition in which bowel movements are passed more often than usual and in a more liquid state than normal.

digestion—The process of breaking down food into simpler chemical compounds that are capable of being absorbed by the intestine.

diverticulitis—An infection in the large intestine caused by the rupture of pouches in the intestinal wall.

diverticulosis—A condition in which small pouches (diverticula) form in the wall of the colon.

duodenum—The first part of the small intestine.

egestion—Elimination of solid waste. It is also called defecation, having a bowel movement, or pooping.

endoscope—A small, flexible tube-like instrument, with a light on the end of it that allows a doctor to see into the esophagus, stomach, duodenum, and colon.

enzyme—A protein that speeds up certain chemical processes. Enzymes are needed to break down many foods into simpler substances so that they can be absorbed.

esophagus—The organ that connects the mouth with the stomach.

feces—Solid body wastes, passed as bowel movements.

fiber—The part of a plant that is not digested. Fiber plays a role in controlling the consistency of feces and the speed at which food is moved through the digestive system.

gallbladder—A sac located beneath the liver that stores bile produced by the liver.

gastroenterologist—A doctor who specializes in treating diseases and disorders of the digestive system.

glucose—The most common simple sugar found in nature.

gluten—A protein in grains such as wheat, rye, barley, and oats that is toxic to people with celiac disease.

hydrochloric acid—A strong acid produced in the stomach that works with pepsin and other enzymes to digest proteins.

ileum—The lowest part or end of the small intestine.

indigestion—A term used to indicate any disruption in the digestive process. Symptoms commonly include heartburn, nausea, bloating, and gas.

ingestion—The process of bringing food into the body— eating and drinking.

jejunum—The section of the small intestine between the duodenum and ileum.

lactase—An intestinal enzyme that is needed to digest lactose.

lactose—A complex sugar found in milk and milk products. Lactose must be broken down into simple sugars to be absorbed.

large intestine—The part of the intestinal tract that extends from the ileum to the anus. The large intestine is divided into the cecum, colon (ascending, transverse, descending, and sigmoid), rectum, and anus.

liver—A large organ located in the upper right section of the abdomen that secretes bile and is involved in the processing, storage, and distribution of many nutrients.

mucosal layer—The surface lining of the digestive organs that protects the organs from being digested themselves, produces enzymes and digestive juices, and in the small intestine, absorbs nutrients. Also called mucosa.

pancreas—A gland located next to the duodenum and behind the stomach that produces juices to digest food.

pepsin—An enzyme produced in the stomach that breaks down protein into simpler molecules.

rectum—The very lower end of the large intestine leading to the anus.

small intestine—The largest part of the digestive system. It connects the stomach to the large intestine. The small intestine is divided into the duodenum, jejunum, and ileum and is the site where most of the digestion and food absorption occurs.

sphincter—A ringlike band of muscle that constricts a passage or closes a natural body opening.

stomach—The large, J-shaped pouch that is found between the esophagus and the small intestine.

stool—The waste matter discharged from the anus, also called feces or poop.

ulcer—An open sore on the skin surface or on a mucous surface such as the lining of the esophagus, stomach, or duodenum.

vagus nerve—A nerve from the part of the brain called the medulla oblongata connected to the stomach that plays a role in the production of stomach acid.

Find Out More

Books

Bjorklund, Ruth. *Food-Borne Illnesses*. New York: Marshall Cavendish Benchmark, 2006.

Byrnie, Faith Hickman. *101 Questions about Food and Digestion That Have Been Eating at You—Until Now*. Brookfield, CT: Twenty-First Century Books, 2002.

Parker, Steve. *Break It Down! The Digestive System*. Chicago: Raintree, 2006.

Walker, Pam and Elaine Wood. *The Digestive System*. San Diego, CA: Lucent Books, 2003.

Web Sites

Human Anatomy Online: Digestive System
http://www.innerbody.com/image/digeov.html

Human Body Adventure: Digestive System
http://vilenski.org/science/humanbody/hb_html/digestivesystem.html

Your Digestive System
http://www.kidshealth.org/kid/htbw/digestive_system.html

Your Digestive System and How It Works
http://digestive.niddk.nih.gov/ddiseases/pubs/yrdd/index.htm

Your Gross & Cool Body: Your Digestive System
http://yucky.discovery.com/noflash/body/pg000126.html

Bibliography

American College of Gastroenterology. http://www.acg.gi.org

Crohn's & Colitis Foundation of America. http://www.ccfa.org

Johnson, Leonard R. *Gastrointestinal Physiology*. Philadelphia, PA: Elsevier Health Sciences, 2006.

Marieb, Elaine N. and Katja Hoehn. "The Digestive System." In *Human Anatomy & Physiology*. Upper Saddle River, NJ: Benjamin Cummings, 2006.

Mayo Clinic Digestive System Center. http://www.mayoclinic.com/health/digestive-system/DG99999

National Digestive Diseases Information Clearinghouse. http://digestive.niddk.nih.gov

Sleisenger, Marvin H., Mark Feldman, and Lawrence S. Friedman. *Sleisenger and Fordtran's Gastrointestinal and Liver Disease: Pathophysiology, Diagnosis, Management*. Philadelphia, PA: Elsevier Health Sciences, 2006.

US National Library of Medicine and the National Institutes of Health: MedlinePlus. "Digestive System. http://www.nlm.nih.gov/medlineplus/digestivesystem.html

Index

Page numbers in **boldface** are illustrations and tables.

About the Author

Gretchen Hoffmann, MS, enjoys learning and writing about many topics in health and science. She has research experience in molecular biology and virology from her work at Boyce Thompson Institute in Ithaca, NY, and holds degrees in Biological Sciences from Cornell University and in Biomedical Journalism from New York University. She currently works as a senior medical writer at a medical education company, where her expertise spans a wide range of therapeutic areas, including infectious disease, nephrology, gastroenterology, cardiology, immunology, diabetes, and oncology. Ms. Hoffmann has written several health-related books for young readers and has also been published in Scholastic's classroom magazine, *Science World*. She lives in New York, with her husband, Bill, and their dog, Rudy.